THE LIFE & TIMES OF

Nelson Mandela

BY
James Brown

SIENA

This is a Siena book
Siena is an imprint of Parragon Book Service Ltd

This edition first published by
Parragon Book Service Ltd in 1996

Parragon Book Service Ltd
Unit 13–17 Avonbridge Trading Estate
Atlantic Road, Avonmouth
Bristol BS11 9QD

Produced by Magpie Books Ltd, London

Illustrations courtesy of: Hulton Deutsch Collection;
Mayibuye Centre; Mirror Syndication International;
London Features International

ISBN 0 75251 546 2

A copy of the British Library Cataloguing in Publication
Data is available from the British Library.

Typeset by Whitelaw & Palmer Ltd, Glasgow

SON OF THE CHIEF

When he was a child, Nelson Mandela was still in touch with a now vanished, and even then fast vanishing, world. When he was born, on 18 July 1918, South Africa was in the hands of Europeans – indeed parts of it had been for centuries. But something of earlier times lived on.

He was the son of Chief Hendry (in some versions Henry) Mgadla Mandela by Nosokeni Fanny, one of his four wives. His great-great-grandfather had been Chief of all the Thembu, although his father was in a

A rondavel, Mandela's childhood home

junior branch of the family, and so inherited none of the most prestigious titles. It is, however, worth remembering that Nelson Mandela, a man possessed of such an innate authority that it would shine through even in prison, is of royal birth.

In his earliest years he lived at Qunu in the Transkei with his sisters and their mother in her three rondavels (small, circular, thatched buildings); they slept in one, cooked in another, and the third held their stores. The name by which he is now generally known was given him one day by a teacher, in honour of Admiral Nelson. His Xhosa name is Rolihlahla, or 'Making Trouble'. As future years would show, there was no end to the trouble he could make in a good cause. But among his family, as he played and helped with the farming, he was known as 'Buti'.

He was not destined to inherit his father's

chieftancy; it would go to a half-brother instead. So his parents determined that he should be educated, but they lacked the resources to send him to school themselves, and in any case Chief Hendry was gravely ill. He therefore appealed to the acting Paramount Chief shortly before he died and in effect gave him young Buti. As Mandela explained in 1977 in a letter: 'Mother could neither read nor write and had no means to send me to school. Yet a member of our clan educated me from the elementary school right up to Fort Hare and never expected any refund. According to our custom, I was his child and his responsibility.'

In the first instance he was sent to Mqekezweni – once the centre of Thembu life. There he shared a rondavel with Justice, the Chief's son. He went to school during the week, and on Sundays to Sunday school – though his father had not been a Christian, his mother was. Of his life outside lessons he recalled, 'I hunted, played sticks, stole mealies on the cob and . . . learnt to scout; it is a world which is gone.'

His people held the merest fraction of the lands that had once been theirs. But something of their old way of life permeated his upbringing, while he learned more about the old days from stories he heard the elders tell. He also learned how that life had been lost. He recollected these days when on trial in 1962:

'Many years ago, when I was a boy brought up in my village in the Transkei, I listened to the elders of the tribe telling stories about the good old days, before the arrival of the white man. Then, our people lived peacefully under the democratic rule of their kings and moved freely and confidently up and down the country without let or hindrance. Then the country was our own. We occupied the land, the forests, the rivers, we extracted the mineral wealth beneath the soil and all the riches of the beautiful land. We set up and operated our own government, we controlled our own armies and we organized our own trade and commerce. The elders would tell tales of the wars fought by our ancestors in defence of the fatherland, as well as the acts of valour by our generals and soldiers during those epic days . . . This is the inspiration which, even today, inspires me in my struggle.'

When he completed primary school, the clan honoured him with a feast and sent him on to the next level of schooling at the High School in Healdtown in the Ciskei. He also progressed within the clan. When sixteen he was sent off for ritual circumcision at the appointed place on the banks of the Bashee river. Later he would recall the lesson he

Nelson Mandela, aged 19

learnt in enduring pain in silence, and the admiration his courage excited. Thenceforward he was accounted a man in his clan. He would have to wait another sixty years before he was accounted a man in the South African state.

He graduated from Healdtown in 1938. There were further celebrations in the clan. The chief gave him his first suit and sent him to study for a degree at Fort Hare, one of the few avenues to university education open to Africans. For a brief period, as profoundly serious men sometimes do, he became something of a dandy. He still dresses elegantly. As a student he was caught up in a vogue for ballroom dancing, and used to break college rules to slip down to the local dance hall. He challenged the authorities in a more serious way when he became involved in a protest over the quality of the institution's food. He was among those sent home. At home more trouble awaited him. His guardian, the Chief, insisted not only that he submit to the Fort Hare authorities, but also decided that he should get married. To make matters easier for him, the bride had already been chosen: a stately young woman of a considerable size. Justice and Nelson decided to flee to Johannesburg, making off with a couple of the chief's oxen to defray their expenses.

These two country boys headed off on a long journey by bus and by train, and arrived at last in the strange urban world. On one reckoning Johannesburg prospered from the Second World War, which even then raged elsewhere. South Africa had no trouble selling its products to, for example, a Britain hungry for resources with which to fight. But though South African industry was doing well, its success then as later was in large measure attributable to its exploitation of cheap, controlled African labourers, who lived in poor, crowded conditions. The boys' only contact in this intimidating world was a fellow clan member, an *induna* (captain) of the very Chief they were fleeing. He worked at the Crown Mines. Honoured to receive these royal guests, he welcomed them and found them work. Mandela became a policeman, guarding the workers' barracks.

The Chief soon tracked them down. His son, Justice, dutifully headed home. His ward, however, decided to stay.

JOHANNESBURG

Life in this huge city was different from anything Mandela had known. He stayed with a succession of families, whose kindness he recalls with affection still. But he must also have felt somewhat bewildered. One neighbour saw in him a pleasant, but rather lost young man, and decided the fiancé of a friend of hers might be the man to help.

The fiancé turned out to be Walter Sisulu. Even then he struck his immediate circle as a highly capable person. His father had abandoned the family, leaving his mother to toil away as a washerwoman to bring up her children and educate them. This she did to such good effect that, at the time Mandela first met him, Walter Sisulu was an estate agent, dealing in such few properties as Africans were allowed to own. He was also a member of the African National Congress (ANC). He took the young Mandela under his wing: he gave him a job, and subsidized the continuation of his studies. He even bought him a suit in which to graduate in 1942.

It was at Walter Sisulu's house that Mandela met Evelyn, his first wife. She was a remote relation of the Sisulus, and had lived with them for a while when she had arrived in Johannesburg in 1939. By her own account she loved him at first sight. A few months later he proposed, and they were married in 1944. They started their married life in a room in her sister's house. Meanwhile he

continued his studies part-time at
Witwatersrand University with Evelyn's help.
When they were allocated a three-room
house of their own, Mandela started to
assume the responsibilities of an elder brother
by supporting and educating one of his sisters.

This period was also formative for him in a
broader sense. He saw how old ways were
breaking down in the new urban situation,
and he encountered a range of responses to
the problems of his people. Segregation was
not rigidly enforced in the universities, and he
had the chance to meet and appreciate people
from a variety of backgrounds and traditions:
European liberals and Marxists; members of
the Natal Indian Congress with a legacy of
non-violence bequeathed them by Mahatma
Gandhi from his years in South Africa. He
was also for a while drawn to hard-line
African Nationalism: Africa for the Africans.
Through Walter Sisulu he joined the ANC.

It was a very different organization in the 1940s from the mass movement it was to become. In some ways it was not even a political party. It had been founded in 1912 by a group of middle-class African men. It cultivated an air of respectability, and sought, in the first instance, only civil rights for Africans, hoping that as the situation evolved political rights would follow. This was not quite so unrealistic as it would have been later. For example, in the Cape, up to 1936, Africans who met a property qualification did indeed have the vote; in that year even that was withdrawn. The ANC Mandela joined in the 1940s retained something of its original ethos of conservative respectability.

He soon involved himself in attempts to make it more radical. He joined the ANC Youth League, and served on its executive committee along with Oliver Tambo and Walter Sisulu. It was founded in 1944, and, led by the brilliant Anton Lembede, espoused African nationalism. Indeed, it criticized the ANC's leader, Dr Xuma, for his willingness to co-operate with non-African groups.

While Mandela subscribed to the Youth League's policy, the seeds of his later rejection of it were already being sown. The struggle of the Indian community had impressed him, as had the multi-racial organization of the South African Communist Party. One incident in particular emphasized how much Africans and non-Africans had in common. He was trying to board a bus with some Indian friends. The Afrikaner conductor told the Indians they could not travel with a 'kaffir'. They sought to engage him in debate; he summoned a policeman. The Indians were promptly arrested and Mandela taken as a witness: technically he had not committed an offence, and provided he testified against his friends he would have been freed. He was having none of this, and demanded that he stand trial with his friends. As it turned out the consequences were not too grave. They were defended by Bram Fischer – the son of a senior judge, which may have helped in securing their acquittal. That he was also a communist and a white man who was a principled and passionate opponent of the white government struck home to Mandela. Indeed, it was the making of a lasting alliance, for Fischer later led the defence team at the Rivonia trial in 1963–4, and was himself subsequently imprisoned for defying the regime.

Reflecting on these and other experiences Mandela came to commit himself to the ideal he holds still of making a new South Africa that will be a fit home for all the races who live in it.

Evelyn

ACTIVISM

From the first the Youth League was more
radical than its parent organization. The mid
to late 1940s were a time of unrest. The
wealth produced by South African industry
was signally failing to enrich the black
workers on whom it depended. The
government responded by outlawing strikes,
but to no avail: they continued. A
particularly large strike by the mineworkers
in 1946 – in spite of the fact that it was
brutally suppressed, with many miners
injured and some killed, and their union
destroyed – reflected the kind of power of

the masses which the Youth League hoped to harness for the ANC.

The League suffered a blow when Anton Lembede died suddenly in 1947. In the resulting reshuffle Mandela became Secretary. But the cause suffered a heavier blow the following year, when the Nationalist Party won the election. They were to remain in power continuously virtually until Mandela himself became President in 1994, and they represented a dangerous mixture of fear and aggression on the part of the majority of the white population that voted them in. The post-war world would see the eclipse of the European colonial empires. Where once it had seemed (however mistakenly) quite normal for a minority of white men to govern millions of others, this now became unacceptable in the world at large. Whereas the British in India or elsewhere in Africa could in the last analysis pack up and go home, the white population of South Africa was far more deeply entrenched, with roots going back to Dutch colonists of the mid-seventeenth century. The Afrikaners, who were descended from the Dutch, were passionately devoted to their land and their independence, and had twice taken on the might of the British Empire to retain them. In the post-war world they became increasingly beleaguered, but their tradition was one of dogged courage in the face of huge odds. Unfortunately the government of the Nationalist Party represented the application of the great qualities of the Afrikaners in a diabolical cause: apartheid, the policy of racial segregation with white domination.

With the possibility of early success snatched away by the Nationalists' victory, in 1949, at the ANC conference in Bloemfontein, the Youth League pressed the ANC to adopt its Programme of Action. The League had reformulated its position to embrace a multi-racial future for South Africa, but even so Dr Xuma refused to support their call for a more radical approach, even though feeling in the conference was running their way. The leaders of the Youth League lacked the experience to be credible rivals to Dr Xuma, so they put their weight behind Dr James Moroka, who was duly elected as leader in Xuma's place. He was not conspicuously more radical than his predecessor, but even so his election represented a change of direction for the ANC. At the same time Walter Sisulu became General Secretary, and Mandela joined the executive committee. The Programme of Action became ANC policy.

There was still some reluctance to make common cause with non-African groups. When in 1950 a May Day national strike was called by the Communist Party, the Natal Indian Congress and the Transvaal ANC, the Youth

League stridently opposed it. Even so the strike commanded sufficient support to unnerve the police, who attacked in force. Nineteen died; over thirty were injured. When a further day of action was scheduled for the following month, the League set aside its objections. The strike enjoyed full ANC support.

Over the next couple of years ANC-sponsored protest increased, with Mandela playing a leading role in his capacity of Volunteer-in-Chief of the Campaign of Defiance, which was run jointly by the ANC and their opposition groups. The Campaign proceeded by identifying certain laws as unjust: those dealing with racial classification and segregation, and the Suppression of Communism Act. First a letter was sent to the Prime Minister requesting their repeal. When that got a predictably unhelpful answer, they set about deliberately breaking these laws in a disciplined, peaceful manner.

Nelson and his son Thembekke

Mandela toured the country tirelessly, enrolling volunteers, and continually contending with the indignities and inconveniences imposed by racist dogma – restrictions on travel and accommodation. Protesters everywhere committed calculated breaches of the pass laws, or marched into the 'Whites Only' sections of, for example, railway stations. Mandela himself was arrested in Johannesburg, having continued to address a meeting beyond the 11.00 p.m. curfew for Africans. He was released, having seen an instance of callousness on the part of the police of a kind that would become grimly familiar: one prisoner was pushed roughly by the policeman and broke his ankle; treatment was denied until the following day.

On 30 July 1950 Mandela was among the leaders arrested under the Suppression of Communism Act. While they were awaiting trial, the campaign spread. As far as the ANC was concerned it was peaceful. But violence was always a possibility, given that the authorities were armed, and might use force either because they were just jumpy, or because they hoped to discredit the opposition with bloodshed. At New Brighton railway station on 18 October, after the alleged theft of some paint, two Africans were shot. Chaos erupted, and more lives were lost: seven Africans and four Europeans. The government, on no very clear evidence, blamed the Campaign of Defiance.

The Campaign was in fact finally brought to a halt in part by internal weaknesses: as the leaders were banned it was unable to organize effectively, and the Campaign lost momentum. But the ANC had made a breakthrough to mass membership.

The leaders, Mandela among them, were tried that November. The President of the

ANC, Dr James Moroka, stood somewhat apart from his colleagues by arranging for his own defence. However, the consequences were not grave for any of them. The judge accepted that the protest had been peaceful, and found them guilty of 'statutory communism', which, as he wryly observed while handing down their nine-month suspended sentences, had 'nothing to do with communism as it is commonly known'.

There was some rearrangement of the ANC's leadership in the wake of the campaign. Dr Moroka's conduct at trial was frowned upon, and that December he was replaced by Chief Albert Lutuli, while Mandela himself became President of the Transvaal ANC, and Lutuli's deputy in the country as a whole.

Meanwhile Mandela had become a father. By the early 1950s his family consisted of two

sons and a daughter, but it had to compete for
his time not just with politics, but also with
his professional commitments. He had
qualified as a lawyer, and in 1952 he set up a
practice with Oliver Tambo. They routinely
overworked as they struggled to deal with
scores of cases of discrimination and
misfortune of a kind which few other lawyers
would handle. The state of South African law
was such that non-whites were readily sucked
into the criminal justice system, and such that,
as Mandela pointed out, heeding one's
conscience often put one at odds with the
law.

Much of the time Mandela was hindered in
his work because he was banned. This was a
punishment which could be inflicted by the
government without reference to a court of
law, so that there was no chance for the
victim to put his case, still less to appeal.
Under the ban imposed on him in 1953

Mandela was confined to Johannesburg, required to quit the ANC, and forbidden to attend to any public meetings. In later years banning orders would become more stringent still. His family, who saw little of him, were sometimes secretly glad of these restrictions that meant he spent more time at home. But shackled as he was, he still found ways to carry on. Unable to attend the conference of the Transvaal ANC, he had his presidential address read to them, thereby sending them a vital message about how to organize themselves from the grassroots up in ways resistant to government interference. This was the 'M' plan: 'M' for Mandela.

The mid to late fifties saw key developments in apartheid itself. The clearance of Africans from Sophiatown, a comparatively pleasant neighbourhood of Johannesburg where they could own freehold property, began in 1953.

It was close to white areas of the city, and having been emptied of its original population, the whites moved in and renamed it 'Triomf'. Even more systematic were policies developed under the aegis of Dr Verwoerd, first as Minister of Native Affairs, and then from 1958 as Prime Minister. He framed the Bantu Education policy (the Nationalist Party called all Africans 'Bantu'). It was explicitly designed to equip Africans for nothing but servitude. Provision of alternative education for Africans was outlawed. He also conceived of the 'Bantustans'. The idea was to herd a large part of the African population into separate areas, which would then become nominally independent. If one set aside the fact that approximately 30 per cent of the population were being crammed into just 13 per cent of the land, and onto territories where they could not sustain themselves economically, this could be made to appear a concession to the 'Bantus'. In practice South Africa could wash its hands of responsibility for millions, while continuing to draw upon them as cheap, controllable labour. The policy was, as Mandela dubbed it, a 'swindle'.

The mid-fifties also saw a significant attempt to regroup on the part of the government's opponents, however. If the government would not hold talks with them, they could at least hold talks with each other. Accordingly, the Congress Alliance convened in 1955 with delegates from the ANC, the Indian Congress, the South African Congress of Trade unions, the Coloured People's Organization, and – a modest but significant group – the white Congress of Democrats. In June 1955 the 2,824 delegates gathered at Kliptown. This vast meeting started one Saturday, somewhat surprisingly, relatively unhindered by the authorities, with Mandela (then banned) attending in disguise. They heard and approved the Freedom Charter, which proclaimed: 'The people shall govern; all national groups shall have equal rights; the people shall share in the country's wealth; the land shall be shared among those who work it; all shall be equal before the law; all shall enjoy equal human rights; there shall be work and security; the doors of learning and of culture shall be opened; there shall be houses, security and comfort; there shall be peace and fellowship.'

The police called on Sunday, gathering evidence of suspected treason, and taking every document in sight, including two signs offering 'Soup with Meat' and 'Soup without Meat', in which the alertly suspicious minds of the detectives contrived to discern treasonable intent. However, the Congress had done is work. The police, even so, continued assiduously to assemble evidence over the next few months.

THE TREASON TRIAL

Eventually at the very end of 1956 the authorities felt ready to strike, and arrested 156 people, Mandela among them. In the intervening period the government had given a perfect example of the counter-productive nature of apartheid. Systematic, if nothing else, it decided to extend the pass system – by which an African needed a pass to get a job, to travel or to be out after curfew – to women, who having formed themselves into the Federation of South African Women in 1954 were not only outraged, but had the organization to mobilize and express their opposition, along with the ANC Women's League. Thus the government made more enemies for itself.

The immediate effect of the government's arrest of so many leaders of the opposition and throwing them all into detention together was another own goal. Many of those arrested were banned, and so unable to communicate freely with each other. Now, thanks to the government having brought them all together, they were able to exchange ideas. However, the occasion was grave: if found guilty, they faced execution.

The trial opened in some confusion as first the microphone failed to work, then the defence successfully objected to the wire cage in which the defendants were penned, and finally the police outside lost control of

A recess during the treason trial

their trigger fingers and injured some twenty people. The trial was to prove uncommonly protracted. It didn't start in earnest until August 1958 – the accused having been granted bail – and lasted in all just over four years, putting those defendants who lasted the course under inhuman pressure.

Mandela was himself able to withstand it, such was his singular strength of personality. But his political work had taken a severe toll on his family life. Evelyn and he had not had much time together, and when she resumed her profession as a nurse and started to train as a midwife, they had even less. Besides this, she was a Jehovah's Witness – something her husband had little chance, and perhaps little inclination, to come to terms with. He was a powerfully charismatic man who kept himself very fit, and was most attractive to

Nelson and Winnie's wedding

women. Under these various pressures the Mandelas separated, and in due course, once the trial was under way, Mandela secured a divorce.

It was in the early stages of the Treason Trial that he met Winnie Nomzamo Madikizela for the first time. She was young and strikingly attractive, and was then a social worker. From the start their relationship was inextricably bound up with Mandela's work. One of her earliest memories is of a walk they took through the countryside, when Mandela asked her to help raise funds for the defence in the Treason Trial. They were married in 1958, once his divorce had come through, in her family's home in Pondoland. Her father reminded his daughter at the ceremony that she should remember that in marrying Nelson Mandela she was committing herself not just to a man, but to a cause. He could scarcely have known quite how true he spoke. The marriage lasted for over thirty years; they would be together for only about three of them.

In Pretoria the trial entered a crucial stage in August 1958. By January of the following year the defence had managed to have the charges against all but thirty of the defendants thrown out. However, Mandela was among those thirty. It was a difficult time for the opposition. On the one hand some Africans, Winnie Mandela's father among them, were prepared to co-operate in the Bantustan policy. On the other, the ANC's policy of multi-racial democracy was challenged from within by hard-line African Nationalists, who eventually broke away to form the Pan-Africanist Congress (PAC). Such disunity weakened the opposition, even though it left the ANC internally more unified.

By the following year, with the Treason Trial still lumbering on, the situation in the country had grown more tense. The British were preparing to pull out of their remaining African colonies – Ghana gained independence at the end of the decade, and many other British African colonies would follow during the sixties. Protests at such things as the forcible uprooting of African communities readily flared into violence. The ANC planned a large-scale campaign against the Pass Laws to start on 31 March 1960, only to have the PAC try to beat them to it by organizing a similar protest for 21 March. The PAC organizers gave strict instructions to their followers to conduct themselves peacefully. At Sharpeville, after a minor fracas in which a policeman was knocked down, the police lost their nerve and fired. Sixty-nine dead; some two hundred injured – most of them shot in the back. A few hours later at Langa near Cape

Town, after giving largely inaudible instructions to the crowd to disperse, the police again resorted to violence: first batons, then guns. Two dead; forty-nine injured.

The country erupted. The government imposed a State of Emergency. On 8 April the ANC was declared an illegal organization. Mandela and his fellow defendants in the treason trial were locked up, and remained so until the State of Emergency was cancelled that August. Oliver Tambo escaped to organize resistance abroad. Such was the tense situation, with the attention of the world focused on South Africa, as the trial proceeded. The state sought to prove that the accused had pursued a policy of violence. In relation to official ANC policy and ANC-sponsored actions, such as the Campaign of Defiance, it failed to do so.

However, the prosecution sought to tease out the alleged implications of statements and articles by the accused; trying to show that in effect the ANC had intentionally sought to bring about a violent confrontation with the government. The trial was just dragging itself into the fifth year when Mr Justice Rumpff cut short Bram Fischer's presentation of the defence, and adjourned for a week. On 29 March the defendants reconvened to hear Mr Rumpff's judgement, suspecting that they were to be found guilty without further ado. He delivered himself of his opinion of the ANC: it was left-wing, but not communist; it did plan to use illegal means of protest; it did plan radically to undermine the state. But on the other hand the accused were not guilty of the charges brought against them: they could go.

Nelson and Winnie after the acquittal

UNDERGROUND

Mandela went straight from the court into underground political activity. In the interval between adjournment and acquittal he had appeared at a vast meeting in Pietermaritzburg to oppose Dr Verwoerd's plan to turn the country into a republic, thus ousting the British monarch as head of state. Verwoerd pushed it through, and on 31 May 1961 South Africa was declared a republic; in the meantime, increasing criticism from other Commonwealth countries led to South Africa's decision to leave the Commonwealth. Mandela continued to mobilize opposition to this move, dodging the security forces as he did so, and earning himself the nickname of the 'Black Pimpernel'. His professional life ceased; he scarcely saw his family; but he did keep the struggle going, occasionally appearing to inspire and help before vanishing again. He laid plans for a three-day strike that May – or rather a 'stay-at-home' since anyone organizing a strike, such as pickets, could be prosecuted. In the teeth of extensive government counter-measures the strike was moderately successful; even so on the second day Mandela decided to call it off, and then set about identifying and dealing with the ANC's shortcomings as a covert organization, as it had now been forced to become.

He was also one of a group within the ANC, though distinct from it, that felt the time had come to reassess the policy of

non-violence. No headway had been made
against a government that had few scruples
about using force. They therefore formed
Umkhonto we Sizwe – 'Spear of the
Nation'. It was decided that, even in the
face of extreme provocation, MK, as
Umkhonto was often known, should strike
only at property. Their hope was that the
foreign investors on whom the South
African economy depended would lose
confidence and withdraw, thus putting
pressure on the government to start to
negotiate peacefully with the disenfranchised majority.

While this was being planned, Mandela
scarcely saw his wife and their children at
all, though he would turn up unexpectedly
on occasion, as once when he appeared just
long enough to buy Winnie a much-
needed new car before melting back into
the crowds. They spent a few short months

The Pietermaritzburg meeting, 1961

together while he was lying low in a small farm rented by the organization. However, more often the struggle came first. He went on steadily building up cells, risking detection as he did so. On one occasion he was sure that the approaching black policeman had recognized him in his chauffeur's disguise. The policeman came closer and closer – surely all was up – then walked past, covertly giving the ANC salute as he brushed by. MK struck its first blows in December 1961, destroying economically and politically significant targets. The following month Mandela secretly slipped out of the country. His mission had several purposes: to raise funds, to establish military training courses for MK's recruits, to lobby for international support, and – a significantly farsighted move – to establish scholarships for young Africans who would one day be needed to help run their country when the struggle had been won. His journey took him first to Ethiopia, then to other African states, on to London, then back to Africa. He received some weapons training himself in Algeria. Finally he slipped back into South Africa, to be debriefed by his colleagues, and receive a rebuke from Chief Lutuli, leader of the ANC. Albert Lutuli had been awarded the Nobel Peace Prize shortly before MK's first strikes, and was dismayed at the abandonment of pacificism, albeit by a group that was not technically part of the ANC. They parted on good terms, however.

Finally, as was bound to happen, on 5 August 1962, Mandela was arrested. He had been disguised as 'David', chauffeur to the theatre director Cecil Williams, but an informer tipped off the police. He was imprisoned in Johannesburg to await trial.

A campaign to free him got swiftly under way. For their part, the authorities made life as awkward as possible. He was transferred to Pretoria, which made it impossible for Joe Slovo to represent him as had been planned. All meetings relating to his case were banned, and so was he, thus making it impossible to appeal to public opinion. The state prosecuted him on two counts: helping to organize the illegal strike of May 1961, and leaving the country without proper travel documents.

Mandela chose to conduct his own defence. He arrived in court in traditional Xhosa dress to the voluble greeting of the public, and started by challenging the right of the court to sit in judgement on him: 'I consider myself neither legally nor morally bound to obey laws made by a parliament in which I have no representation. In a political trial such as this one, which

Nelson Mandela in tribal dress

involves a clash of the aspirations of the African people and those of whites, the country's courts, as presently constituted, cannot be impartial and fair.'

His line of argument was rejected, and he was required to plead to the charges. He pleaded not guilty. In the ensuing trial he showed that he had sought peaceful discussions with the authorities before calling for the strike. Even so, it was hard to deny that he had promoted the strike and that he had travelled without official documents. He concluded with a final submission to the judge, which was unquestionably true in all save a technical legal sense: 'Your worship, I submit that I am guilty of no crime.' The court then found him guilty. His final plea in mitigation of sentence was a formidable, impassioned and dignified statement of political faith, and he finished by promising to resume the struggle at the earliest opportunity. On 6 November the UN voted in favour of sanctions against South Africa. The following day Mandela was sentenced to five years' hard labour – a sentence which he began by sewing mail bags in Pretoria Central Prison.

THE RIVONIA TRIAL

He was soon transferred to the notorious Robben Island, just off Cape Town, and a natural prison – indeed the Dutch had used it as such in the seventeenth century. In the country at large the conflict between the government and the people worsened. John Vorster, as Minister for Justice, had introduced 90 days' detention without trial. This could be renewed to the grave. For some this was literally true: in September 1963 Looksmart Solwandle Ngudle became the first political prisoner to die in police custody.

With Walter Sisulu on Robben Island

That July the police captured key figures of
the opposition in their secret refuge in
Rivonia, near Johannesburg. It was part of a
broader crackdown against dissidents of
various kinds, which led to simultaneous
trials in different parts of the country.
Mandela was hauled out of prison to stand
trial with Walter Sisulu, Govan Mbeki and
Ahmed Kathrada, among others, on various
charges of sabotage and related crimes, in
what became known as the Rivonia Trial.

The defence team, led by Bram Fischer,
laboured under various handicaps – not
least the government's announcement that
the accused were guilty, though of what
exactly remained unclear because details of
the charges were not revealed for some
time. It would be an achievement for
Fischer and his team to save the lives of the
defendants. That said, things started well for
them. There was something about a system

as irrational as apartheid that sometimes
seems to have impaired the intelligence of
those who ran it. The initial charges were
framed in so slipshod a manner – even
managing to accuse Mandela of assisting in
crimes that occurred while he was in prison
– that Fischer made hay of them, and the
judge threw the case out. Not to be
defeated by their own incompetence,
however, the authorities instantly rearrested
the accused and hauled them off to the
cells.

The trial resumed on 3 December 1963.
That the accused would be found guilty in
the end was scarcely in doubt. The revised
charges covered 193 counts, which in effect
added up to treason, although that was not
the crime with which they were specifically
charged. The defence conceded twenty
charges, but this did not detract from the
moral authority of Mandela 's plea, repeated

by his fellows, 'The government should be in the dock, not me. I plead not guilty.'

The state loaded the dice against them. Their witnesses included informers and liars. The authorities also bugged the defendants' consultations with their lawyers, which meant that important messages had to be written to each other, and then burnt in an ashtray. This was wearisomely inconvenient, but it led to an amusing incident when Mandela, noticing that the notorious Lieutenant Swanepoel was prowling about in the doorway, with great seriousness passed a note to one of the lawyers. The lawyer read it gravely and with deliberate slowness, crumpled it and prepared to burn it. Swanepoel dashed in muttering something about the risk of fire, and seized the note, only to find that it read: 'Isn't Swanepoel a fine-looking chap?'

As if they didn't have problems enough,

Bram Fischer's defence team also had to contend with the fact that their clients were more concerned with establishing the truth and the moral justification for their actions than with saving their own lives. While the lawyers had nightmares about executions, Mandela calmly courted death and remained unstintingly cheerful as he did so. On one occasion, when the authorities forced the defendants to consult with their lawyers in a room whose partition made it resemble an ice-cream parlour, Mandela beamed through the glass and asked, 'What will it be today, gentlemen, chocolate or vanilla?' – to the annoyance of the police colonel who no doubt expected the defendants to be discomfited by the new arrangement.

Finally in April 1964 the defence opened their side of the case. Winnie Mandela and Mandela's mother looked on as Mandela delivered a statement from the dock concerning the history of the struggle. He spoke of the ANC's history of non-violent struggle, of the need to take more radical measures in the face of state violence, of MK's commitment not to kill; and then of the relation of communism to the ANC, and the distinction between them; and finally of the political and economic hardships suffered by the African people. He concluded: 'During my lifetime I have dedicated myself to this struggle of the African people. I have fought against white domination, and I have fought against black domination. I have cherished the ideal of a democratic and free society in which all persons live together in harmony and with equal opportunities. It is an ideal which I hope to live for and to achieve. But if needs be it is an ideal for which I am prepared to die.'

The trial then proceeded, focusing on

others of the accused. In the midst of all this Mandela was imperturbably continuing with his studies, and in fact sat London University exams in law just before the verdict was delivered in June. Of the nine accused, all save Lionel Bernstein – one of the two remaining white defendants – were found guilty. Sentence would be passed the following day. The attention of the world was on South Africa. The UN had demanded the release of the accused; newspapers outside South Africa seconded the call. The judge claimed to be influenced only by the circumstance that the state had chosen not to charge them with High Treason as such, though the crimes of which they had been found guilty amounted to it. They were to be imprisoned for life.

PRISON 1964–1990

All of them, except Dennis Goldberg, who as a white was imprisoned elsewhere, were sent to Robben Island. It was the last the world would see of Mandela until his release in 1990.

Conditions were harsh. As political leaders they were held in isolation from other prisoners. Having requested that they be allowed to do some useful work, by day they laboured, breaking rocks or building a new cell block. By night they froze in clothes that were no protection against the cold off the Cape. From the first Mandela sustained himself by struggling to have their complaints taken seriously. Come the summer, they were ordered to toil in a lime quarry; it was a suntrap in which they baked. Once in six months they were allowed to send a letter and receive a non-contact visit of half an hour. Scarcely less punishing than this prison itself was the anxiety Mandela felt for his wife, left to bring up their young family alone, and ceaselessly harassed by the authorities.

Ignorance or anxiety about what was going on outside was a part of imprisonment. They were not allowed newspapers, since the prison authorities wanted to control their knowledge of what was going on outside.

Their first hint that Dr Verwoerd had been assassinated in September 1966 was the increased harshness of the warders. In 1967 Chief Albert Lutuli was killed on a railway line under suspicious circumstances. In 1968 Mandela's mother suffered a fatal heart attack; he was not allowed to attend the funeral. Heavy blows fell the following year when Winnie Mandela was arrested, and held for five months, during which she was tortured. She was brought to trial, found not guilty, and immediately rearrested. She spent nearly 500 days in solitary confinement, without having been found guilty of anything. So far from apologizing, the government served her with a banning order, and soon arrested her for breaking it. A couple of months after his wife's first arrest Mandela was told of the death of Thembi, his eldest son, in a car accident. According to fellow prisoners he withdrew into himself, refusing to burden them with his personal problems. As ever, bad news (and sometimes misinformation) reached the prisoners quickly enough.

Apartheid looked depressingly secure from the mid-sixties onwards. Internal opposition had been crushed, while many neighbouring states were sympathetic: Mozambique and Angola were Portuguese colonies; Rhodesia (now Zimbabwe) was ruled by a white minority; South Africa itself ruled Namibia. B. J. Vorster had succeeded Dr Verwoerd as Prime Minister. By nature highly authoritarian, he enjoyed a power base in the security forces, and looked unshakeable.

Then from the mid-seventies the situation started to change. In 1975 Mozambique and Angola gained their independence. In 1979 the Lancaster House conference, which would finally end white minority

rule in Rhodesia, convened in London.
Within South Africa there was renewed
unrest. The trade unions acquired a new
importance, and were able to organize
strikes. In 1976 in Soweto the government
faced opposition from black schoolchildren
who objected to the imposition of
Afrikaans as the language of the schooling.
As their campaign spread, the government
reacted in characteristic fashion: between
June 1976 and the following February, 575
people were killed; over a hundred of them
were children. A generation missed out on
their education in the collapse of anything
approximating to normal life. Winnie
Mandela, having been imprisoned again in
1974 and 1976, lent her support to the
schoolchildren's campaign. In 1977 she was
condemned, without trial, to internal exile
in Brandfort, a small place in a hard-line
Afrikaner district in the Orange Free State.
Grim as this was, she was more fortunate

than some. Steve Biko is perhaps the best-known of an increasing number of Africans to die in police custody.

A few months after Mandela's sixtieth birthday Vorster fell from power in the wake of a corruption scandal, and was replaced by P. W. Botha, another leading politician with a power base in the security forces. He recognized that formidable problems confronted him. Determined to maintain white supremacy, he combined hard-line repression with an attempt to make allies of the Indians, the Coloureds and the non-white middle class generally. The latter part of the policy culminated in the new constitution of 1984 which gave Coloureds and Indians a vote, but only to elect representatives to an assembly other than the white parliament, where power continued to lie. The resulting tricameral system won little support. At the same time military spending soared: the military budget in 1985 was almost seven times what it had been a decade earlier. Force was used not only inside the country's borders, but also outside them, as the National Party sought to annihilate and assassinate its enemies. While the government resorted to bloody terrorism, the MK continued its work of sabotage.

The situation appeared to be approaching its crisis. Botha's attempts at reform were undermined by the ruthlessness of the other plank of his policy. Although the world boycott of South African industry was never wholly effective, the diversion of huge resources into the armed forces and loss of confidence among overseas investors took their toll on the economy. At the same time, the internal political opposition organized itself into the United Democratic Front – a gathering of many groups

Zinzi Mandela

reminiscent of the Congress of 1955. It
staged a huge rally in August 1983.
Mandela managed to smuggle a message
out which was read to another UDF
meeting, in Soweto in 1985, by his
daughter Zinzi.

Contrary to the hopes of his captors,
Mandela had never been forgotten. A
campaign to free him had gathered
momentum, not just in South Africa, but
around the world. The government itself
toyed with the idea of releasing him, but on
their own terms. In 1973 he had been
offered release provided that he live in and
recognize the 'Bantustan' of the Transkei,
so eager was the government to gain some
legitimacy for the Bantustan policy. The
offer was repeated with particular insistency
in the mid-eighties. By then, as part of the
complex game in which the government
hoped to use their best-known political

prisoners as pawns, Mandela and his fellows had been transferred from Robben Island to Pollsmoor Prison on the mainland, where, with certain exceptions, conditions were somewhat better. But Mandela's answer to the government's overtures was in effect always the one his daughter relayed to the UDF rally in 1985: 'Only free men can negotiate. Prisoners cannot enter into contracts.'

In this impasse, and with the added problem that the Nationalist Party's support was leaking away to the far right, Botha declared a State of Emergency. Government violence and repression raked the country. At the same time it was clear that Mandela would be central to any lasting solution. From inside prison, and unseen by the world at large for over two decades, he had achieved the position of a world statesman. Even as a prisoner his air of command was impressive. Lord Bethell, who visited him in Pollsmoor in 1983, was so struck by his natural authority, even when surrounded by the very warders who were guarding him, that it took him a moment to realize that he was in fact meeting Mandela himself, and not some senior official. One of Mandela's warders was won over: Sergeant Gregory had been wholly opposed to him and his cause when he first encountered him on Robben Island, but became a loyal admirer.

In 1988, shortly after the world had celebrated Mandela's seventieth birthday, he had to go into hospital to be treated for tuberculosis. Once he had recovered, he was taken to live in a warder's cottage at Victor Verster Prison, with a separate establishment under the direction of Warrant Officer (as he had by then become) Gregory. Here he could receive visitors more freely – indeed the whole family could come.

He was also on one occasion able to pay a visit – to P. W. Botha himself. Postponed because of Botha's stroke in January 1989, the meeting between the two men finally took place at the State President's official residence in July. It proved surprisingly pleasant, but inconclusive. The following September, with Botha still in poor health, his cabinet replaced him with F. W. De Klerk. De Klerk was ready to contemplate whatever it would take to break the deadlock. The following month some of Mandela's fellow political prisoners, including Walter Sisulu and Ahmed Kathrada, were freed. Early in February 1990 the ANC and other banned organizations were unbanned. In an atmosphere of celebration and anticipation the eyes of the world turned to Victor

Verster Prison. On 11 February 1990 the world finally set eyes on Nelson Mandela once again.

Addressing a vast crowd, 1990

PRESIDENT MANDELA

Mandela's freedom gave hope for a peaceful settlement, but it was still a long way off. When he met the crowd that gathered in Cape Town he gave De Klerk credit for the steps he had taken, but reminded the world that apartheid was still in place. He resumed public life with impressive assurance. After a reunion with Oliver Tambo, the ANC's President-in-exile, it was established that he should become Deputy President of the ANC.

He faced intractable problems. While the

government was willing to talk, it was far
from willing simply to abandon power and
it still had formidable forces. In the country
at large a culture of violence had taken hold
in some quarters. Many young Africans had
missed out on their education, and were
disgruntled by Mandela telling them to go
back to school. Violence raged on. The
police killed eleven protesters in March
1990, and soon afterwards – a grim
indication of problems to come – Zulu
Chief Buthelezi's Inkatha party attacked the
ANC in Natal.

The world was eager to see Mandela, and
he set off on journeys at a ferocious pace.
He wanted to thank those who had helped
to put pressure on the regime, but also to
enjoin them not to slacken their efforts just
yet. He was fêted wherever he went. New
York accorded him a tickertape parade; in
Washington he addressed the Congress; a

rock concert was held in his honour in London; in Paris President Mitterand received him with elaborate ceremony, while the crowds cheered.

Back in South Africa the government had begun to hold talks with the ANC, but they were dogged by violence outside the conference room which threatened whatever progress had been made within it. Ostensibly much of this violence was tribal, often Zulu against Xhosa. But there were suspicions that the authorities were at best culpably lax about bringing the culprits to justice, and at worst conniving with them in the hope of benefiting from unrest. Mandela claimed that the violence was fuelled by a sinister third force in the security services. The death toll mounted; hopes waned.

In July 1991 Mandela succeeded the ailing

Nelson with Oliver Tambo

Oliver Tambo as President of the ANC. Under his aegis the ANC delegation participated in the first round of the CODESA (COnvention for a DEmocratic South Africa) talks at the end of that year. But they stalled, with neither the PAC nor Chief Buthelezi taking part, and Mandela and President De Klerk at loggerheads. An increasingly beleaguered De Klerk was having to contend on the one hand with earlier revelations tending to substantiate suspicions about the third force of agents provocateurs in the security services, as Mandela had contended, and on the other with the leakage of support to the far right, to the Conservative Party and Eugene Terre Blanche's AWB (Afrikaanse Weerstandsbeweging – Afrikaner Resistance Movement) in particular. Determined to consolidate his position, he took the risk of calling a referendum on his policy of negotiation. In the event, with the support

Winnie

of the Liberals, he won handsomely. But from the point of view of the disenfranchised majority it was another vote from which they were excluded, and which lacked its pretended authority to settle the fate of the country.

Meanwhile Mandela had to address painful circumstances surrounding his wife. She had supported him selflessly during his years of imprisonment, and suffered greatly herself. Yet almost from the time of his release it seemed that personally, and to some degree politically, they had grown apart. She had fallen in love with a younger man, Dali Mpofu. Not only that, but she had become caught up in the endemic violence. In 1991 she was found guilty of kidnapping and of being an accessory to assault in connection with the killing of Stompie Moeketsi, though later on appeal the second charge was quashed. Colleagues paid tribute to her earlier work and sufferings, but for many she was a discredited figure. Yet Mandela felt guilt over the plight in which she had been left when he was in prison, and could not forget the selfless loyalty with which she had supported him. For a while he loyally stood by her, but he was in an impossible position. Finally on 13 April 1992 in a dignified statement he announced their separation.

Later that year the CODESA talks resumed. They had no sooner started than violence erupted again. Mandela could scarcely support talks with the government, while his own people were being killed, apparently with the tacit support of elements in the security forces. The talks ground to a halt. The stalemate lasted for several months. The ANC mobilized mass support to put pressure on the government

President Nelson Mandela with Deputy President F. W. de Klerk

with strikes and marches. The government suffered from further revelations about the nefarious activities of its own forces. An ANC march in the Bantustan of Ciskei ended in violence and death. The negotiations were on the verge of breaking down irreparably. Only a summit meeting between Mandela and President De Klerk pulled them back from the brink, while both sides kept some contact going out of the public gaze, and an outline agreement was pieced together, with the so-called 'sunset clause' guaranteeing multi-party government for a period after elections to be held early in 1994. This agreement was promptly imperilled by the assassination of Chris Hani by a member of the far right AWB. Hani had been destined for high office, and could have played a vital role in rallying radicals in the ANC to support compromise. His death triggered panic. For three nights running Mandela appeared on television calling for order – in itself indicative of where real authority then lay in South Africa. As if the assassination were not enough, the AWB then attacked CODESA itself, charging into the building in which the talks were held with an armoured car. Even so, in June 1993 a date was set for the country's first fully democratic election: 27 April 1994.

At last Mandela felt he could call for the lifting of sanctions. For a while there was amity, at least between President De Klerk and himself, who jointly received the Nobel Peace Prize in December. In the same month South Africa's first multi-racial government, the Transitional Executive Council, took over. However, the extreme right and Inkatha were unhappy. The AWB invaded the Bantustan of Bophuthatswana to support the tyranny of its president, Lucas Mangope, but they

Queen Elizabeth talks to President Mandela and his niece

were defeated when the army went over to the people. The AWB then embarked on terrorism with a series of car bombs, culminating in one at Jan Smuts airport. Finally the police tracked them down to a farm in the Transvaal and arrested them. Also unnerving in the panicky state of the country, and indicative of it, was the bloody manner in which ANC security guards warded off a Zulu protest march from their building in Johannesburg.

Even so, electioneering continued, with Inkatha finally joining in at so late a stage that the ballot forms had to be amended at the last minute to include them. When election day itself finally came, not surprisingly, a system that had never had to cope with so many voters groaned under the strain. But suddenly a spirit of exultation seized the land, and what could have become a frustrating and dangerous business went off with remarkable good humour that augured well for the new South Africa.

As expected, the ANC emerged as much the biggest party. On 2 May President De Klerk conceded defeat. In the first general election in which he had ever participated, Mandela had become President. He was sworn in on 10 May, with his Deputy Presidents, Thabo Mbeki and F. W. De Klerk.

Enormous problems confronted, and still confront, President Mandela's government: widespread poverty, high unemployment; and while apartheid may be dead, it is a disease with unpleasant after-effects, and maintaining racial harmony – or at least keeping racial disharmony to a minimum – is a demanding task. Inevitably the euphoria of the election itself wore off, though something of its spirit was revived with the Springboks' spectacular victory in the Rugby World Cup in 1995, urged on by their President. Less colourful but more important is the encouragement of the rest of the world with the lifting of trade sanctions, and the Republic's rejoining of the Commonwealth. So, although the road is long, at least it leads the right way.

Nkosi Sikelel' iAfrika
God bless Africa

Acknowledgements: This little book is particularly indebted to Mary Benson's *Nelson Mandela,* a lucid account of Mandela's life, now revised to include the 1994 election, and to Fatima Meer's life of Mandela, *Higher than Hope.*